QUEEN'S GATE

PIA TAFDRUP was born in 1952 in Copenhagen. Her first collection, *When an Angel Breaks Her Silence*, was published in Denmark in 1981. Her fourth book, *Spring Tide*, was published in English by Forest in 1989. In 1991 she published a celebrated statement of her poetics, *Walking Over Water*. Pia Tafdrup received the 1999 Nordic Council Literature Prize – Scandinavia's most prestigious literary award – for *Queen's Gate*. Her poems have also been translated into Swedish, German, French, Portuguese, Spanish, Italian, Dutch, Macedonian, Romanian, Slovenian, Slovakian, Russian, Turkish, Hebrew and Arabic.

PIA TAFDRUP

Queen's Gate

translated by
DAVID McDUFF

BLOODAXE BOOKS

ISBN: 1 85224 567 0

First published 2001 by
Bloodaxe Books Ltd,
Highgreen,
Tarset,
Northumberland NE48 1RP.

www.bloodaxebooks.com
For further information about Bloodaxe titles
please visit our website or write to
the above address for a catalogue.

Bloodaxe Books Ltd acknowledges
the financial assistance of Northern Arts.

northern
arts

Cover printing by J. Thomson Colour Printers Ltd, Glasgow.

Printed in Great Britain by
Cromwell Press Ltd, Trowbridge, Wiltshire.

ACKNOWLEDGEMENTS

Queen's Gate was first published as *Dronningeporten* by Gyldendal, Copenhagen, in 1998. It won the 1999 Nordic Council Literature Prize, and its publication in English has been assisted with a translation grant from the Nordic Council. Some of David McDuff's translations of poems from *Queen's Gate* have previously appeared in *Danish Literary Magazine* and *Gods and Mortals: Modern Poems on Classical Myths* (Oxford University Press, 2001).

CONTENTS

I

The Drop

My Mother's Hand

Bathing in a drop's quiet light
I remember how I came into being:
A pencil stuck in my hand,
my mother's cool hand around mine, it was warm.
– And then we wrote
in and out between coral reefs,
an undersea alphabet of arches and apexes
of snail-shell spirals, of starfish points,
of gesticulating octopus arms,
of cave vaults and rock formations.
Letters that vibrated and found their way,
dizzy over the white.
Words like flat fish that flapped
and dug themselves into the sand
or swaying sea anemones with hundreds of threads
in quiet motion at the same time.
Sentences like streams of fish
that grew fins and rose,
grew wings and moved in a rhythm,
throbbing like my blood, that blindly
beat stars against the heart's night sky,
when I saw that her hand had let mine go,
that I had long since written myself out of her grasp.

In

In through
a snow-open gate
I have come.

At my back
the wind squalls
sharply from the northernmost sea.

A house I will build,
a poem from the lightning snow,
milled from the sky in a homeless flood.

It will stand like a flame of frost
and the air around
will be glass-clear and easy to breathe.

A space for the folding mountains of the mind,
a place of refuge for longings
and hibernated dreams.

A territory
where cries from the heart's ice-bird
are transformed into song.

Faster than the words
are shaped in my mouth,
my thoughts pile up in great blocks.

I think with each flake
that hurtles alones and plunges
Icarus-like down from heaven towards me.

I hear the snow growing, construct
from falling particles white music
played without mercy to the deaf.

Don't know the word's final place
in the order of future sentences,
until I catch a flake on my tongue.

Listen myself warm
and let it melt to a drop,
a black and white image filled with colours.

Cast a third look, linger and judge,
let the drop freeze to ice again
to raise it into a constellation.

I slow the tempo,
make time unfold
ever more slowly.

Can't remember en route
who are the living and who are the dead,
don't know tomorrow, but remember yesterday.

In through
a snow-open gate
the road leads to the poem.

Pain Light

It has rained, and a drop catches the light now,
breaking it inaudibly into a prism,
as it pivots in ascension
on the tip of a grass-blade like a foetus
rocked into its first dream.
The drop quenches thirst or laves a wound,
the drop, an ocean for micro-organisms,
a shadow pearl in the grass in fog and grey weather,
acid flash in the eye, making colours turn
to transfixing white in the sun,
from the exiled moment
when over the abyss of five senses
it gathers the morning's silence or sinks
like a star through me.
The drop may be met by another drop,
not so that one plus one makes two,
but to fuse into one larger.
The drop keeps its secret,
heavier than its own weight,
At any second it can be loose and elastic:
Make a cup overflow, or
fall to the ground with a sound
like that of a single syllable –

Nature Morte

In the vase flowers that collapsed
on the way home in a taxi, on the dish
fruits drowned in their own juice,
skulls and hip sockets full
of brooding twilight, echo from a life's
reading rooms, siren calls and warnings.
A bowl of tears, a jug
of buried laughter, the first kiss,
a never-opened casket, a nest
robbed of its birds' eggs. And feathers,
seething feathers from Icarus' wing,
many nights locked up without sleep
beneath a hermetic heavenly vault.
A candle burned down, a loaded pen
pushed by waking dreams, papers
that have gathered grains of dust
that long danced in the sun's rays,
broken down bookshelves and children
poured out with water from the bath,
an interminable score for leaping whales
whose wild song rises
from the depths of the sea towards the sun,
drop by drop, blood-happy moments.

Voices, Tracks

Blood-shadow, night-crystal,
lungs filled
by a winter's glittering.

I stop
where the earth has pushed naked stones
through its shell of frost.

The dead
send their light
upwards into the spring, ice-white.

Cast their radiance
across the deserts of the soul
like hidden voices.

The world is made for those
who in their wilderness
can dream Another...

In that thin layer of snow, dazzlingly extended,
I follow the drop-shaped tracks of an animal
in between the tree-trunks of the woods and out again.

Towards a wild sea of light on the horizon
I walk, it is the voices
and the tracks in the snow that call in chorus.

And you who, searching from your place,
now come to meet me, have also followed
the drop-shaped tracks of an animal.

Have also roamed about alone,
as if the route were laid
by a conductor's baton in the air.

For a Change

No two hailstones hurtle
identically through a spherical space,
no two snowflakes are the same.

All these twins in my mirror,
they come into view from a past
with numbers tattooed on their arms.

Examined and selected
for medical experiments,
disease injections and silent glowing incisions.

Through the same blood-steeped gate
they have come, but only in language
do they look alike as two drops of water.

They do not have the same soul,
each one awaits from the night
a catapult for flying dreams.

An unopened grave lies ready,
regardless of whether we are shot, hanged
or end as living torches.

Language says 'dead',
but no two people die
the same death.

With crystal-hard tenderness
I scrape the words free of dust
down to the last remnant of meaning.

I drink the air,
breathe black and deep, air my inner being
to sing pure and firm as an unknown sea.

Hatshepsut In Memoriam

It is so simple to blast
out of the cliff's rock
a gigantic block of stone,
a small wedge of wood
and a few drops of water.

As simple as erecting
an obelisk of bird–
dreams captured in
their mass of stone,
the brain will be formed intelligent.

As simple as a leap
in language and sudden as birth–
water flows, the desert's
sand is bound with stars
into one attentive kingdom.

II

The Lake

Arrival

A lake that shines, a lake that opens, a space enclosed
by trees all round, by lapwings in the air and the smell of August,
a stillness full of cries from birds and splashes of fish in the water.

A lake that wakens, bulrushes and reeds rustle in the inlet,
where great hordes of titmice hide, and ducks chatter
from a carpet thickly woven from the oval heart-shaped leaves of
      water-lilies.

The tongue tries the fresh seawater, it tastes bitter of metal;
a breeze strokes the skin, sets its riffled imprints on the water,
feathers and grass drift away, dragonflies hang low in the sun.

A pair of swans dive from the air, brake with a hissing,
glide out inspecting more sharply than the man and the woman
who took turns guarding Rembrandt's 'The Night Watchman'.

The moment's light-play in the water, where fish plough the darkness,
but suddenly come close in fits and starts, more and more of them,
short thrashes with their bodies, before they leap across the mirror.

A smell of life and rot and eternity oozes up from the lake,
where plants sway like sleepwalkers, and the bottom
lies like the depths of a cave, a dream captured in its own form.

A lake of fire, a lake that burns, as though it had swallowed a heart,
and the one who comes down to the lake sinks to the bottom in his
      own body,
is at home there and nowhere else.

Frost Hall Meditation

Motionless up here beneath the winter sky, scattered spruces and pines,
birch trees rest without the slightest stirring, when the cold rawly
hacks its sword through the throat, cuts its way to the bronchial tubes.

A layer of snow has laid itself to rest on the frozen earth, paper thin,
in the valley the ice closes the lake,
while a smarting in the lungs gathers to the point of nausea.

At the foot of the mountain sounds the brook,
that still flows freely under the ice further away
and calls the silence in this frost hall more clearly forth.

Like thoughts that are loosened from the wall of the brain,
the snow cracks glass-like when footsteps approach the railing,
where the cliff falls steepest.

I listen to the water far below,
to the language, whose accent, even in the wildest fever-sleep
is recognised as the mother's speech.

The cold glows and shoots
its needle points into my cheeks, sprouting fire
frost-brands the skin for life.

The silence grows, becomes so much more powerful than an explosion
that thoughts amassed through years suddenly hurl themselves over the
             railing,
roll down the mountain amidst uprooted trunks, scrub and lichen-clad stones.

Break the ice on the lake amidst clumps of silent spruce to sink
down into the darkness and mud on the bottom, perhaps strike roots in
             the spring
beneath insects that dance on outstretched wings in moist air.

And again heave themselves from the depths as yellow waterlilies, blaze
             sky-bright
as torches, if you are lured down there in summer
by elongated, restless shadows over the water.

A Place in the Snow

The earth's crust stiffens, biting frost forms encircles
the lake, turns it within a few nights
into a place in the forest, a sudden point of transition –
an unexpected naked surface to find a foothold on,
but hard as stars.

Snow falls quietly like a freshly shaken quilt round someone who
        is sick,
like the first wild kisses pressed
against strange, fragrant skin under an unbuttoned shirt;
the snow lies and hides the lake's darkness, covers the scars
that time engraved, figures of pain each with their story:

For example the scissors that opened,
scissors that entered the flesh, with the same crisp, crackling sound
as when poultry is cut open,
to make the birth-opening wider,
issue a visa for a journey into the world.

All the sounds of the summer have withered and vanished,
the shadows stopped, sated, like the wind, by the universe,
die down among the trunks of century-old trees,
the sun comes out, the winter light's diamond dazzles the eye,
the lake lies like a wing splayed out at my feet.

I move across the snowed-up ice,
a hidden mirror for the slow insight
that keeps the sky outstretched;
snow falls quietly, I step into a zone,
untouched and open to new impressions.

Don't brood on yourself, go over the whiteness –
go away over the fish in the lake
and their realm of undeciphered, swarming signs,
spermatically scattered in the darkness,
a sleep-thin layer of ice crystal separates you from death.

Make your way across the ice, as you stumble down the paper,
a space in time will open from thought to sound,
close your eyes, absorb not only the words,
but also the whiteness from within and carefully, don't wake anyone,
it's all right to dream deeply as you lay your tracks.

Mythic Morning

It was a morning captured by the dew,
white, but transparent and in April now.
Quite without warning there the garden was
galactically covered in a wakeful gleam
with pillared trunks around the water's edge,
where birds rose upwards to the sky or sang
from willow-shots, from birch-screen, undergrowth,
from green beech and exquisite copper red,
but all the trees as yet were still in bud.

The new, fresh grass shot up along the shore
from last year's pale and withered blades,
and nothing moved the rushes and the reeds.
It was an unknown day, when water lay
so dreamlike, shiny in the oval lake.
A riot of anemones crept down
the slope, down quiet to the water, down
to pilewort roots that stood like lightning bolts,
while stinging nettles showed their notches' awls.

It was a morning filled with humid air,
it was a lake so black, as if it hid
a cruel hoard of pain down on its bed.
It was a morning captured by the dew,
green, but transparent and in April now,
a morning when you had to touch with feet
the old lawn's tautened net of moss
and feel the earth enveloped and recall
the way it yielded joyfully and soft.

It was a Nordic Fujiyama where
you had to feel the earth, the air so near,
and where you felt like walking in a trance
across the grass down to the lake to see
and smell the mud and marsh from lake-bed mire,
and watch the water stand so chilly there,
that even smallest fish en route to light
like drops of rain that rose from underneath,
could break the mirror's calmness now with ease.

It was a room, it was a moment, too,
when seed desired to blindly meet the egg.
It was a morning captured by the dew,
wet, but transparent and in April now.
From trees around the water, singing came,
where garden birds sat up on branches, high,
like still-warm hearts impaled upon a stake.
Who vanished here, they vanished without trace,
and no one then would see a weightless flight.

It was a spherical, unearthly place,
a patch that seemed an idyll now and then,
but dark's night in the soul accompanied.
Within this beauty there were wounds and scars,
it was like someone pointing with a hint
at some wild, strangely simple game,
a greater power, unseen, that intervened,
a death found everywhere, and even in
the day's hello there was a farewell pang.

But it was winter woken from a sleep,
it was a morning wrapped in insight's light,
transparent, filled with an eternal time.
It was a lake that with its eye could see,
it was a water that was magnet-like.
It was a day where new wings rose
into the air to draw out whiplash trails
and dart like shadow over water there,
cross heaven's space with all the speed of joy.

The Mirror's Optics

I would like to go down to the lake at midsummer
in the light that holds memory secure,
draw breath amidst the sounds of birds
and song of timber being cut,
amidst wind and the dying of wind,
light and shadow, flies and humming midges,
amidst ants by circuitous routes
approaching their hill, and snails
gluing their way through the grass.

I would hear the water suck and splash under the boat
that is moored at a jetty of fragrant pine planks,
be marked by the wind when it moves in the trees around the lake,
tugs at clumps of reeds along the edge,
pulls at the myrtle shrubs that well out over the water,
when it knocks birds down from the tops,
hear it take hold of yew and birch,
young rowan trees and oak thickets,
grass and ferns that grow thickly everywhere.

I would cast a stolen glance at the box full of carefully chosen hooks,
while the boy on the jetty doesn't catch anything,
and dark clouds move across the sky,
where the sun at long intervals
finds an opening and breaks through for a few seconds,
and the boy, whose heart is thumping loudly,
waits for a bite, as if his life depended on a cast,
as though his happiness were fixed to the end of the line on the hook,
jiggled through the worms that squirm in the air in pairs.

I would follow that boy who has a skin of stone,
the one who hardens and casts the line again,
while the sun comes and goes, and the water gleams,
a minefield for stored dreams,
I would see the lake lying as before
with its indomitable bird island,
with the bonfire site that looks smaller year by year,
but is still there like the benches and the boat
that rocks with the oars drawn up in the rowlocks.

I would feel annoyed about a strutting electricity pylon
towering above the forest in the distance, quite naked,
where a silver-gleaming train, shiny as the back of a fish,
shoots past far in among the spruce trees
along a plane different from the time
that reigns by the lake, to which I come
because it does not come to me –
and where the sun suddenly crashes out of a cloud
so the light chasing back into my eyes makes me dizzy.

In the optics of the water's mirror I would see the time
when all tracks led to the lake, down to our hidden spring,
the time we talked our way through sunny summers, hung on
to the stream of words, while fish on their splayed-out fins
deep down in the sky's abyss floated
over darkly amassed, green-brown stones, greasy to step on,
the time when we bathed from warm rocks in the gasping cold lake
or caught fish after fish, which we cooked on the fire,
the time when the night, when it lay on our eyes, did not weigh
        us down.

Now the summer is cold and full of clouds,
when we come through the thicket to the lake alone
or together without exchanging a word,
not because we are stopped by something invisible,
like a wasp behind a pane of glass on its way through the summer,
but we listen differently to the merciless wind in the trees,
to the black chopping blows of the waves against the boat
and try to reconcile ourselves to the thought
that a place gives its best nourishment to those who leave it.

Signs of Fate

By the lake on a grey day when it's about to rain,
and the wind rides past on its journey,
and the cold creeps in under your skin,
when you are tormented by someone who is jealous
at the moment of the flood,
where the darkness over the lake grows and grows,
the way that skin changes colour,
and the water begins to look like tarnished silver,
when the smell of lake water hangs in the damp air,
as penetrating as animal secretions
or day-old sperm,
when the swallows fly low so to seize a diving insect
in one swoop
the second before it drowns among the smallest animals,
that flake like light through the water
seek shelter among the lake's swaying plants,
a colony of weightlessly drifting creatures,
when the shininess is perforated
and the water is pierced by drops that sting,
as consciousness is woken from its barbed-wire sleep,
when the lake's surface is veiled like that mirror
in which you look at yourself: Banished
from the story you would so much like to have been part of
by showing a different face from your own
– if degrees of pain could be remembered
we were never without a fever –
by the lake when a shower, like a wave driven by the wind,
sweeps over the water like a deep breath,
week-long downpours when the walls of heaven come crashing
        down,
and the lake in the grey flickering light
is turned to a metal plate blasted
by a sawn-off shotgun: bullet-
holes scattered in their own
universal semantic order
like the many lost acres of the soul come together
to form a panic of meaning – patterns
not always legible to those who are wounded themselves,

signs of fate in uninterrupted combinations,
which perhaps – who knows – unfold at a greater distance
like floating flowers of light in the blackness,
stars that never rest.

Wannsee

A sigh through the lofty treetops as soft
as a heap of ashes lifted by the wind, light
as the hearts of birds beneath the sky.
The night an open pulse; breathe deeper –
time they keep, the trees, ring upon ring.

Ineluctable as opened pages
of documents for evacuations
and later deportations by train from Europe's cities,
ineluctable as protocols with columns of names,
long as black flames.

The wound has not yet healed,
though cleansed and pure
it does not stink of infection,
simply in the most extreme loneliness
does not cover the abyss.

The way earth or sand,
thrown over mass graves
with winter snow added on,
do not erase the sight of the dead
or chase thoughts to flight.

Mingle blood with the night, listen
to the quiet water near the trees,
the damp grass smells raw
between sleeping stones and tree-trunks
whitewashed by moonlight.

They heard the same music
from an earlier time of greatness,
the executioners and their victims,
read the same masterpieces,
but each distinguished his language:

One for annihilation, one for continued hope
and of this common possession
again each his own interpretation:
one that was final, and one
that acclaimed the many possibilities.

But when the graves were to be dug,
the victims dug them themselves,
something that can be spoken of
with human language,
but never understood.

The water in slow movement towards the shore,
a star the size of a hand's palm
is reflected yellow in Wannsee.
The region of memory is six-pointed,
searching forward in all directions.

III

The River

The Ice in the Canals

My gaze glides over the frozen canals, Europe shivers,
Rembrandt's mother warms her hands over a brazier.
Boats dart out in the first thaw, where sluice-gates are opened again,
it is the open water between floes of ice that catches my eyes,
it is the brown-green depths that suck my gaze to them.
At night I hear the ice break in a zigzag-hollow rumbling, I stare
under thick blocks of ice into a glittering black continent.
The floes bob in the water, creak and press heavily towards sleep,
rise in glass-steep flames to topple over on one another
or be torn with a crash into enormous star splinters,
tottering shards from the sky's winter mirror.
Sharp-ground are the pieces that cut hard into my dreams,
I sway in my sleep, am grazed, sway naked in the current,
where under a floe of ice I wanted to hide something from others,
but the floe has moved and can't be distinguished from the rest,
which surround me and float on under bridge after bridge.
What I wanted to hide in the dream I can no longer see,
it has been deposited somewhere like songs one clearly remembered
        as a child,
but are now only recognised if they are heard hummed by someone else.
The ice groans in the nocturnal light from the brain's exposed sun,
the ice melts and breaks, and under the rasping floes in the canal
waits a spring where the trees along the bank, like the blue sky,
when the clouds are scattered by rising wing-beats, will be mirrored
        in water again.

The Autumn Distended

And behold, there came up out of the river
seven well favoured kine and fat-fleshed;
and they fed in a meadow.
GENESIS 41, 2

The rivers have quietly overflowed their banks,
along which reeds and thickets and moss-grown tree-trunks stand in water,
newborn spruces compete in swimming strokes with one another.

Winter-sown fields lie like extended lakes that are not sucked up
but reflect the sky with trails of jet planes, parallel ejaculated stripes
          of frost
sign the sky where it plunges into those two planes.

Motionless in winter coats is a flock of red-brown heifers newly risen,
where the black mud meets the wet green,
in a long gust steaming breath wafts from the cattle out into the cold air.

Further south it has rained for weeks without cease, torrents pulse
          and grow,
burst dikes as pain leaps through a body, flood towns and
hide streets and the cars in the streets, bear the carcases of animals.

Water gushes into gardens, gets through barricaded doors and windows,
knocks houses over or surges into basements, rises several storeys,
people sail in the streets, row from house to house, carry hundreds of dead.

I wade across the ploughed fields, up the hill, my feet
slip in the clayey earth, stumble over the furrows on my way;
the tree at the top flies upwards to fetch birds down from the sky.

A colony of rooks lands on the naked branches, hooked like fingers
that for years have practised Haydn's unpredictabilities,
with long cries the birds draw a cloth tightly over the earth.

They drag a shroud of darkness after them, but the sky will be lit up
for a while yet and before that the clouds slide over into a bloody pink
          primordial light,
the white jet trails turn to steely grey before they dissolve.

The sky opens deeply in copper fire, in turquoise, in glowing
        shades of blue,
a space for continued wonder to the opened eye, a ravine
to vanish silently in across the marshy earth.

Sleep Code

The head sinks with all its weight against the pillow,
and above the earth rises the house, whose one windowpane now
has caught the moon in its orbit,
the house hovers with the water that courses through pipes and
      radiators,
a river that rises and flows through the night.

The head ducks and presses itself down into the pillow,
while thoughts dig up the day that has gone,
to rediscover in the ruins sounds of voices
that like drizzle, hidden, weave in across one another
or lose themselves each in its own direction.

The head burrows further into the pillow,
as an animal works its way down into the sand,
the river rises through the room, through the night,
where the body long ago sought rest,
and the head, too, tries to follow after.

The head is suffused by blood,
the blood sings, the river,
the river sings in the head,
which between two heartbeats listens and can't escape the sound
– an 'ee' or an 'oo', that goes on sounding.

Through delta upon delta,
through a self-created jungle of memories,
a root network deeply ramified,
through porous layers of images derived from the soul's innermost
      room,
the night's insomniacs are led with the current.

Drift out on the open sea, on which they
– far away from that crevice
where as a spring the river
leapt from the earth –
will meet, there, where falling asleep is not possible.

And cross one another before the light of morning gleams naked,
so that their filtered webs of thoughts will silently
for a moment illuminate the horizon together,
and the code that activates sleep's reactor
will be remembered again.

Seven Nights and Seven Days

Far inside the night we sail on the river,
the silence spreads out like circles in the air.
We wake up: Palm-trees sharpen against a dawning day,
date plantations cut themselves free of the mist,
like fields of sugar-cane,
fields of clover and horse-beans.
Villages become visible,
pumping stations and sleeping donkeys,
wells, canals, roaming dogs with dusty coats,
mud-built houses with flat roofs, and ruins of the same,
huts made from dried palm-leaves
for the animals in the burning midday sun.
Hordes of domesticated cattle drink from the river, children
bathe and play with their echoes, birds
seek shelter in the reeds, the hooked roots of trees
lean thirst-tensed out over the river.
The water has woken the desert
in eruptions of green on both banks.
Behind the edge of the dark green
rest glaring expanses of fine-grained sand,
an utterly naked desert
where the sound of a heartbeat
spreads for miles, where the air
is reflected in the sunshine like dazzling lakes,
no differently blue from the eyes of a newborn child,
among weathered rocks and fossilised remains
of burnt-smelling wood from what
was a living forest, a desert
where myriads of stars at night
come quite close to touch the one
who stands thoughtless in the sand with neck craned back.

Far into the day we sail on the river,
water buffalo wade along the bank on low meadows
with cakes of dried mud in their skin.
Black-dressed women sit in dense clusters
in the shade of mulberry fig trees, men
cultivate the slopes, they fish and lay nets
out in the river, lads pull boats up on land

or unload at a dragging pace, boys
tend jumping flocks of goats and sheep.
The sky is touched by the water,
a golden chain in the light,
the wildfire of a flute, slow legato.
The monotonous drone of the ship's engine
settles beneath the sounds from inside the villages,
pulverises the lowing of cattle and water buffalo,
the cockerels' screeching and the dryly bleating goats.
The river courses through lakes,
flows through centuries,
like the pulse of sleep under a fontanel,
slowly spelt out and with calligraphically executed signs
like melted-down insects,
peacefully printed on the innermost interior of consciousness.
The sun warms, it gleams
in the river's eddies, a ring dance of light,
its lightning beams glide into the veins,
shine long and without a cloud.
Herons and kingfishers
fly low across the mirror of the water,
shadows drink from the river.

Far into the night we sail on the river, far into the day,
seven nights around full moon
and seven days we go gliding away.
Like a dream-thin thread through the land
the river stretches from south to north,
where it divides again and again
in order to become a delta near the sea.
It courses under concrete bridges, continues in sluices,
into whose chambers we glide in order to wait
for the water-level to fall to that of the river's mirror.
The river sounds like the voice
that is heard behind many years' different poems,
the voice that at a distance makes them flow together
into one long sentence, simple and unquenchable
and completes the silence, when not a ripple
is sensed on the water, and no bird calls.
The river is an album leafed through, a fan
that with one movement of the hand
unfolds into a refined fragrance-realm of remembered life.

The river wakens the desert around it,
as our tongues keep love alive,
the head turns heavily and obliquely backward,
into a space where wings not known before are put to use.

Far into the night we sail on the river,
while the water is faintly lit by the moon.
Expanses deserted as emptied sepulchres
are hidden in uttermost darkness
among scattered electric lights on the bank.
Swell beats on the hull in gentle lappings
when ships pass one another.
We cross the river, breast against breast,
the skin has got its light of crystal from evening-red clouds,
we cross the darkness and each other.
The river is singing silk beneath us,
it has only one desire:
To flow freely as our bodies
as they are licked smooth and in frivolous positions
add yet one more movement to the world.
The river completes each vibration of the flesh,
it leaves our enemies lying like stones on the bottom.
We hear the water, see it sparkle black,
a sarcophagus of basalt.
We cross time, drink summer from winter,
we are without roots, live in a moment of pure movement,
explore the life that is allotted to us before death.
Above us the Milky Way flows at the speed of stars
like a reflection of the river's light curves.
The river is strength and rest at the same time,
and into my river you must descend
more than once –
I see your face lighten out here in the midst of the water,
see your eyes give light to the darkness.

Far into the night we sail on the river,
clouds drift under the moon.
We sleep on the water, we are borne away,
while the images of dreams seek us,
and everything can be dreamt
under the horizon's circle of shooting stars.

The ship is swarmed round by birds
when we run aground,
but after a while we are free again; the oceans
have not yet been filled
by the rivers that, all round the world, flow and flow.

As Long as the Water Is Carried Away

It is not my life that has become liquid, but the willows',
whose roots suck and drink from a fertile darkness,
from the slopes they lean over the running water,
where fish find their way in under the branches' shadow,
the fish stay in the same spot on the river,
while reeds nod the late summer in,
and moss rocks swaying over stones at the edge of the water.

The birds are heard, not only as a filtered net of voices
drawn over the trees, the individual birds become gradually clearer,
one stands out from the others and calls, another answers,
a third bird arrives, the first moves inward among the branches,
the second does the same, before it answers, the third flies
out of the leaves' shadow and away, and also the second,
the first remains, calling loudly from a branch in an arc above the water.

Each sound has its beginning and end, its limits of presence,
more and more birds can be distinguished from one another, until
          distant voices
of children fishing in the river blend upward from a bridge;
first your face appeared in the dream as someone
I recognised among many I had not seen before,
then your voice was heard, as it woke me in the middle of the day,
then again you vanished without having been here.

Or perhaps I was not able to perceive you, as you sat by the river
in the same place I have sat these many last hours
under a birch tree, where light and shadow alternate:
Changes take place perhaps in the fraction of a second
when the eye closes in a blink, for suddenly in the midst of the
          summer's heat
the tree releases its first dying leaf
and lets it fall into my lap, yellow –

The back is warmed in the sun's flicker, the body is time,
time in flesh and blood, the hair lifted by a gentle breeze
while the river, the pale green, greyish river
now streams with cold fish, which without leaving a trace

swim away with shining fins
or are caught up from the bridge by a child,
who suddenly holds his breath – and pulls.

Because you disappeared, long before I found you,
perhaps you will come back,
perhaps you will be there,
as the river is there, as long as the water moves,
only when the river dries into to a flat and stony bed,
where the mud bottom cracks and crumbles,
is it no longer a river.

The wind carries a leaf through the air, the birds sing,
the meaningful takes place at each moment,
it is simply more than we have room for;
the water flows quietly, the wind caresses the back of the neck,
no one becomes one with the many, each is his own,
I close my eyes, I open them,
did you not vanish, did you perhaps not exist at all.

Passage

Through the open window I hear far below
the water invade the summer night,
I set the words in motion like the water,
they move freely, and what strength there is
in a foaming river, what peace, too,
in a language that newborn
explores the universe of the brain.

A river that bends like the wild animal's back
in its familiar terrain, a river
that undulates between the trees
like a loved body, a language
that flows lightly through the landscape
in different stages of consciousness, an alphabet
that glides over the silent earth.

The distant sounds from the river can be heard
like the animal's tongue as it licks or the music
that was there already before we were born
and remind us that the river
is a dizziness beneath us,
a smell, a sound, a dance of flames,
a cool blessing like snow in summer.

The river runs from night to break of day
and night again, it flows
not like a war that is ended by peace,
before a new war breaks out
with violence and exterminations
and charts of absence
with shadows older than ourselves.

But with changes so minimal
that they are scarcely noticeable
and yet accumulate, as the family
is ramified in new constellations,
or the starry trail of words
spinning forms a galactic way
far above the paper, that snow-white avalanche.

As the mother's and the daughter's lives
are joined invisibly to each other
– for the daughter with a dim beginning,
for the mother with a vague ending –
and when the daughter as a child
hears her mother's grandmother tell stories,
the past is nearly without origin.

Since the grandmother remembers her grandmother,
who again remembers –
a queen's path is laid
from yesterday to today and on to tomorrow,
an eternal moment in which distance melts down,
the further we go in sharpened listening,
and the voice is the season that does not change.

Our lives do not hang together
like brick and mortar in the houses along the river,
but as a space in the mind, like one long recollection,
a repeated addition, without anything now
being as it once was,
like the river we listen to
and share across time.

Another kind of prism
from a space telescope
is the glint of remembering,
as if we do not forget the family
because in dreams
weightless
we can greet the dead:

I walk into their hallway,
where the door stands open,
I hesitate, but am met by a beam of light,
when I look for one newly dead,
a light so strong and white
as if the whole depth of the sky
were gathered in this room –

I am a weak link in the chain,
and the river is merciless
for one who wants to turn around,
a sleepless flow, a single outstretched wave,
as if the voice cannot find its way back to the throat,
but in the play of shadows over the water
I know my innermost place.

I continue the life of the family, as the blood
passes from heart-valve to heart-valve,
as the water drifts onwards
and is at home everywhere,
it flows with a sound of its own,
strangely quiet, strangely monotone,
a nocturnal silken way, a whispering from one ear to the other.

The Shining River

He maketh me to lie down in green pastures:
he leadeth me beside the still waters.
He restoreth my soul
        PSALM 23

Clear is the water, blue as in a flame,
like a sky that floats,
the river-bottom rippled and white.
Fine clay lies deposited, almost putty-like
to squelch up between toes,
the white separate from the blue,
the fixed from the flowing.

Quietly the water sets off,
the gaze moves from the depths
up to the surface
and further up over the water.
It is a river of melted snow that runs,
smooth as the muscle fibre of veins,
a river that shines between low cliffs.

Softly single grains of sand are whirled
up from the bottom,
then more and more.
They rise like pillars of smoke
from a wick, when a candle has burned down,
like powder that is mingled in the water from below
and turns it to mud.

Far away belongings can be felt
as they drift ever closer,
where the river widens.
Recognisable tables and chairs,
which once had their own fixed place,
meander in measured procession
between pieces of the dead person's clothing.

Objects that now only furnish
the furthest corners of memory,
are brought down by the river between fields and meadows,
carried away without time.
Only by colour, stream
and silence
as after birds that have flown.

The blue transparent is permeated
by the bone-white
and milky.
Is it a shadow of the sky, bound
that seeks up towards the light,
or is it the living person who is drawn down,
the single being who has disappeared from the crowd?

Clear is the water like one more answer
to questions that invalidate the question,
clear is the water, blue as in a flame,
as questions that invalidate
the answer's question.
Slowly the river flows in sun
– From water you have come.

IV

The Well

The Spring

I write to lift the stone, to waken worms,
snails and other crawling things, write to open a sealed gate
to the light, the water and the ice-blue sky, an entrance sensed
even before it appeared in the maze of dreams.

Hymn and elegy spring from a common alphabet,
the same letters spread black as a network of veins
from skin to skin, while the pen's point shines like gold
in the earth, over which silence vaults in an ever larger dome.

In the way that the sun plays on the water in a shimmer of colours,
the soul is the secret imprint reflected under what is written;
I write and open the gate ajar, just
enough of a crack so that the one who wants to see can see.

A spring that cannot be drained runs out into the well,
where I fill my pen in order to let the night flow
across the paper, that bell of snow where they sound, the words
that line by line hurl me closer and closer to my death.

The Acacia Valley

Here an undercurrent gathers,
here is a well with water
for the plants that withered sulphur yellow
or curled up hopelessly
in dust-grey tints before the summer's death,
to the scorched grass that audibly
whispers in the wind,
to the fields where the harvest failed
and the creatures still cry.

Here is a well
where you can drink
or drown,
fetch a star
from the bottom, slake
your thirst
in the colour white.

Here is a well
that makes the ground-water
behind all mountain-blue thoughts
rise clear again
and the migrated birds
return in great flocks
from far away.

You can concentrate for hours,
light candles in the twilight, attain
those two seconds
of privileged insight
it will take years to forget again:

A gigantic spring will water the acacia valley of consciousness.

Parable

A net cast round the night:
Stars fall through its fine meshes,
the landscape breathes, the stones gather dew,
trees of sleep bow towards the sand.
The sound of the water runs like a voice
through the stillness here,
where a tongue somewhere above my back
makes my heart radiant.
And wakes me slowly from that dream,
where I dreamed that I dreamt
and did not want to wake up from a dream,
where I lay and dreamt
that I was walking round and round a lake.
The tongue licks hoar frost from the wings,
I float, turn around,
notice your smell and lightly caress
your skin, that ascetic garment
spun around the soul like letters,
woven densely out across the paper.
You embrace me, many-armed,
so hard that I grow a heart on both sides;
it is the light I carry in this throne room,
with all your weight over me.
The morning sky is dizzy blue
and nothing has disappeared while I slept.
I fasten my sandal, cross the threshold,
my foot is white in the sand.
I travel through centuries
to a spring where the light trickles.

Joseph in the Pit

Who will listen, who will judge?
Father, you sent me to Shechem,
but my brothers had moved on from there,
I found them at last in a field in Dothan.

I ran and ran to bring back word,
until I saw my brothers, who were feeding their flocks,
my sun, my moon, my eleven stars,
I was a planet in constant movement between you.

Why did you envy me my path?
Why did you mock me for my dreams?
They came to me, without my having called,
when we had bound sheaves or fed the flocks together.

It is completely silent here, the heat increases, the stones sweat,
the smell of my own sun-foreign skin surrounds me,
You conspired to kill me, but on hearing Reuben's words fell
on different thoughts, you took my coat, the one I had been given
                by my father.

The cattle watched us as out in the field you shouted loudly to one
                another,
took hold of my garments and tore the coat from me, so you could say
I had been eaten by wild animals; you lowered me down here,
But there is no water at the bottom of this pit.

Did you, my elder brothers, cast me living to the grave,
when you tore my coat from me and bound me like a sheaf?
I heard you long, made out faintly amidst cicadas
some of your voices as you ate your meal in the shadow of the tree.

Father, in my dream your sheaf bowed to mine, as we bound them,
Mother, yours did also, what do you know of me now, what do you fear?
Brothers, all of you, whose sheaves bowed in the same dream,
where did you go when you later moved on after your meal in the field.

Is this the entrance to the realm of death? Here it is resoundingly quiet,
I am covered by sunlight, bone-white and blinding, the sun is at its
    zenith,
my lips find it ever harder to shape the words,
Father, you love me, and because of that my brothers bear a grudge.

I am alone in my body, cannot see my own shadow,
the flies stick to my neck and my arms, I am sticky
as resin and dates, I long for a drink of water and the wind
I ran against when I was sent away from Hebron's valley.

Brothers, you did not put the cover back over the pit,
did you want to hide me or drown me like an enemy?
Can my cries climb up these crumbling walls,
an arduous journey, can they reach out of this depth?

My pulse reverberates inside this circle of rocky stone,
will I soil these walls from fear before then,
will I be captured naked in the cobweb of my own dreams,
I am not loved by my own brothers.

It will become night down here at the bottom of the well,
and it will become day, is the cistern old and cracked,
may the abyss open and water force its way open,
will rain fall suddenly and violently?

Or will the birds dive after me into this shaft,
will they flap their wings and sink their claws deep into my flesh,
will a beak peck the salt out of my entrails
and drink of my blood as if it were refreshing rain?

If the miraculous happens, if dew falls,
I will lick every drop of it from these stones, inhale their smell
as if it were nard and cassia, almond flower and aloe,
brothers, I beseeched you, but you would not listen.

Am I a slaughtered animal, a sacrificial victim on its way to the altar
or is it the morning sun flowing? Did my words
reach high up above the topmost brim of stone,
did someone after all hear my cries, or was it my prayers?

Does that distant murmuring come from outside or within,
can I make out strangers' voices, or is it me
who calls, calls the ear, or hears the mouth,
do I seek, or am I found?

Am I drowning in my own hoarse shouts,
is it them that fill the well and give the echoes,
will I be fetched out by a passer-by, travelling past by chance,
or is it a final whispering from my own larynx that I sense?

This is not death, you would not shed the family's blood,
it is suffering, the most extreme trial, in which clear-sightedly
and hated I must be a witness to my own humiliation,
but I did not choose my birth, and the dreams came of themselves.

Father, can you tell an animal's blood from my own?
Do I come before my rent and bloodstained coat?
That is what troubles me most of all, that you will mourn
and fear me dead – but death has not yet touched me.

What is it that is coming from my mouth,
am I choking, or am I being cut free from myself?
Do I hear my own voice, or is it really others',
will I reach up over the edge of the pit before my final strength is gone?

No, it is not rainwater that fills the depths of the well,
but the hope of resurrection; I awaken to the voices of a whole caravan,
the rumbling, heavy steps of camels, I am lifted, I am fetched
by travelling merchants, up from this prison, out of the earth's driest
    womb.

The Profile of Memory

suspiciendo despicio
despiciendo suspicio
TYCHO BRAHE

At the bottom of the well the star shines in the water
like an eye that comes into view between clouds in the night.
I lean over the stone brim, a smell
of cold windfall fruit in frosted grass
comes up from the depths, a smell of glowing sex.

The star waits in the metallic blackness,
as though it possessed a knowledge of the life
that lay before the one who is looking.
I lean further out across myself,
my thoughts quickly focus on a jet of blood.

I look into the eye as though that alien gaze might
cast its light into the shadow bird
that keeps on hovering in my inner being.
As if for a brief moment someone else might
break the seal and illumine my past.

Far down the eye entices, it shines wakefully, bottomless,
but does not seek the one who tries to catch it.
As once I hung from a womb, I hang
over an open grave with my face turned towards the water
though I will never be able to read my own face.

The star in the well raises the sky, as if it recognised
a dream: the star shines like the head of the newborn child
before its body – still enclosed by warmth – follows after.
The bloodily smeared head, a solitary globe in the universe,
still nameless, but bearing an echo of centuries.

Kiss the Prince

From the moat sings a chorus of princes,
with her kiss they turned into frogs.
Now they crawl nimbly around among the plants in the water,
roam about along the bank
or sit drowsily on the same spot
with their broad, flat heads above the water
and their powerful hind-legs spread out wide.

They croak up to the castle's red brick walls,
on light summer evenings drown out all other sounds.
Their skin has turned deep olive green with dark spots,
their bellies yellowish white,
the smooth and warm has become cold and nubret,
and from glands in their white skin they excrete a fluid
that faintly smells of onion.

Completely naked they review their youth
when none of them perceived the beauty of the individual woman
for all the women, while one night flowed together
with the next in wine, in kisses, in laughter
and hour-long caresses.
They smiled in dreams and exchanged their names,
which they mumbled to her in their sleep.

They climb around on their domain,
the muddy slope, and open wide their large,
mobile eyes with gold monocles
up towards the stars,
while with their concert
among many names they try to distinguish
– Clara, Katya, Kraka.

From her window high in the tower she hears them repeat
the same notes half the night.
They try hard to remember
what her name is, and they call,
but among the many random names
they blurt out with raised foreparts
she does not hear her own.

In the daytime she delights in the gluttonous amphibians
when they consume their food:
Insects, spiders and snails,
prey which they catch striding along on their forelegs,
by hurling out their tongues like arrows,
on which the small creature is left hanging in sticky mucus,
next to be swallowed whole.

On her walks around the castle shortly before twilight
the warty creatures leap towards her in long bounds
or swim quickly to meet her,
only a few anxious ones plunge into the depths;
the frogs are hard to kill,
they can tolerate mutilation for up to several hours.
Hers is the power and revenge in solitude.

The Horse's Eye

With a neighing in the stall
the horse tugs at the chain,
then struts peacefully again.

A deep black sky is its eye,
in which I am reflected in a red coat
– I stand in there, in the shiny wetness.

While the horse's dreams
fall into a trot and move my soul
out into the light, out onto open land.

To a damp meadow where the sound of hooves
dies away in the grass, cool
as that icon-green colour.

The heart's pulse-beat down here,
where the grass and the earth take me
into the foaming green, where I will not say no.

V

The Sea

The Pen

Whether it is the ships and the cargo boats laden to bursting point
– that all day long sail past my east-turned windows,
where a morning-glowing sun makes its spurts of flame
go chasing into my heart –
that at night cause me to dream
of a swelling penis so beautiful
that I have to touch it, or
whether it is a forgotten sea that has invaded my pen
and now flows through its point
in order to make me write something other than what
I had imagined, I don't know –
but I hereby send my apologies
to the harbour town whose night sky
I, deflowered by light and sound and smells,
destroyed with most unsuitable dreams
fetched up from an ink-black jungle
I did not know I had deep down in myself,
where I naively – I realise it – imagined
everything was as shiny as the lance
that pushes its way into the word's kernel of crystal,
and not shaped like the waves
that now part and gather into a furious
plaiting of sand and water and foam,
into a link that is loosened and locked tight,
waves that knock me over in a caress
and lick across the shore, tongues that chase
and in the sand reflect beginning and return.

At the Far End of the Pier

Walk from the becalmed centre of town to the wind in the harbour,
down to the quay and the smell of tar, out onto the pier to the tall
       lighthouse
I see at night, when I am flayed out of sleep by unknown sounds,
as the skin is pulled from a fish in one jerk
after the head has been severed with a crack and thrown away.

Like an invasion from an alien planet
the seaweed lies washed up on the coast, stinking and bluish black
in foam-marbled sand between scattered bits of rock,
a thick ridge of extinguished life, a vanquished phalanx
dried in the sun until it resembles something mummy-like.

Along the quay and on the pier men are pulling nets up from the water,
and lowering them back into bails with creaking metal wires,
on an afternoon fathers are teaching sons to fish with these nets,
which domed, like inverted parachutes in simple lever stands,
are fastened to the quay or towed out onto the pier in light carts.

Small fish that flicker like autumn leaves in the wind
are gathered up from the nets and thrown back into the sea,
groups of smaller children play in the sand or on a floating dock
from which they launch boats with paper sails
laden with hopes of reaching foreign lands.

Waves replace waves, as doubts are annulled by more doubts,
the sun wanders away over the water starting from the opposite coast,
the light approaches quickly, the colour changes from greyish green to
       olive green,
while the wind and the smell of salt are the same, and the pier breaks
       the waves,
before, raised, they lean in and close around their curvature.

Great waves are thrown in towards the quay when coasters and
       supertankers
glide past or cargo boats steer out of the harbour and sweep away,
glide like shuttles in a loom, like heavy birds without wingbeats,
resting in themselves under the open vault of the sky,
bound for other continents.

The buoys rock scattered in the water- yellow, red and green,
the same ones that pulse their warning light at night,
far away between tongues of land the open sea can be seen,
flowing out into a yearning to sail away
in order to find out for oneself what there is on the other side.

In the bay behind everything is still, the houses stand unchangingly
with their black slate roofs like a secure shelter for dreams,
which are dissolved neither by storm nor rain,
the air cleanses, the conch shells' murmur is blood white,
and within a few days one's skin is ground as clean as a stone
over several years.

Let the wind pass through marrow and bone out on the pier's
furthest point
– do not ask yourself what you are doing here, or what cloth
the ships are weaving for you, you are simply here, rinse off the
fish's blood,
and eat what is caught, are alone with yourself and the Lord
and the dogs roaming around the quay.

You are here to open yourself, to let the time go slowly,
watch the clouds glide over the sky and the strip of mussel shells
grow day by day along the shore
– perhaps end as a pillar of salt at the far end of the pier,
because you looked back the one time in your life you should have
looked forward.

The Smell

The smell, but especially the taste of an oyster,
that silky, wildly virginal, wet creature
served in a basket of ice and sleep-green seaweed,
squeezed on with drops of fresh lemon
and sucked straight from its shell,
is perhaps the nearest I will get
to consuming the seas divine inner being
the easily dissolved soup cube of salty oceans
that demands to be thinned
with bottles of champagne or exquisite white wine
– glass after glass, which also evokes another
and extremely characteristic aspect of oceans:
An alternately cold and warm undercurrent of well-being
that leaves me hanging somewhere in the air,
ready to fly and closer to death,
among seagulls that grap some bread
thrown to them in flight,
already on their way sideways,
towards a swaying horizon, quietly
borne by the wind into the vaulted blue:
Give us this day our daily adventure.

After a Winter's Sleep

Suddenly the moon is high above the water,
carried along by Chopin's nocturnes
coming from a radio in the background.
Gleaming like a winter breast in the first spring sun,
it has come into view, full, between clouds,
which have been rent like a folded cloth
in a single jerk to expose its surface.
It rises slowly high above the sea,
that sluices in a perpetual boiling stream,
waves roll foaming and smack against great stones,
slap and murmur in between them,
a pure bubbling Babel
or meaningful words that can be spelt by anyone.

The water seethes, froths, lies still,
my skin is receptive to the light, the air
and the words that are being whispered here,
as if one night I have been stroked
by a hand whose warmth has opened all my pores,
what an otherwise merely mild summery breeze
would dare when it laid itself over me,
so that all feeling would gather in my sex
and not leave me in any doubt
that without water we cannot live –

How many ships go past
while the hand caresses, I have no idea.
Still less do I know where they come from
or are sailing to, with what cargo
and under what flag,
I only notice my body awaken near the sea
after its league-long winter sleep.

Beginnings can be lived in for a long time,
they have no hands, like the clock I look up at,
a large electric clock encased in black metal.
Both hands have torn themselves free of the round dial
and lie rattling lengthwise between 5 and 7
when I carefully lift the clock down from the wall.
Meanwhile the water outside the windows
has quietly risen and fallen again
in a slow but certain heartbeat.

Wet Desert

As cows graze undisturbed,
flocks of godwit wander over the sandbar,
pecking in rich mire for larvae, crustaceans and small worms.

The low water between shore and sandbar is shiny and still,
only jelly-fish smack along the coast, orange brown and blueish purple,
before they are washed up, and dry into thin membranes.

At the edge of the shore wet tracks of birds and people can be seen,
signs mingling with one another in the velvet-soft sand,
as if they had walked side by side.

All prints that are cast at ebb-tide lead towards the water,
the wind is heard gently, and the waves that follow their own law,
while the head is dazed by the salt in the air when the lungs are filled.

I hear the sea, don't hear the sea,
thoughts are conquered by space or filtered ambiguously
into one another, as fish wriggle in the net when it's drawn up.

The greyness tones so greyly out across the water,
that the body dozes off immediately,
the familiar is wiped out, the soundless grows in strength.

The greyness is a fluid that is diluted by the air,
it settles like a membrane about the convolution of the brain,
wraps them in a light haze of mist.

I am woken by a puff of breath or like a fall from inside and out
preserved at the same temperature as from months before the birth,
hear pulse-beats in the temple.

Everything is as before, only the number of species is reduced,
some birds belonged to another age, another climate,
and don't come any more, while others are on their way.

Like the breath in the back of its neck a woodcock hurries
away over the wet desert, plunges its beak in the sand,
quick as the needle of a sewing machine dives into the cloth.

Other birds move the point of balance, change direction, follow after
like a cry of triumph already before victory, as they spurt across the
                sandy flats
where placenta-sized jellyfish now float like pulsating flowers.

A sea-nettle's vaulted shield is curled at the water's edge to a bell,
is twisted up again and opens, so that garland-like fringes are exposed
and vibrating tentacles cautiously expand the space.

The greyness envelops the soul in a veil, lighter than needle-fine rain,
the waves wash quietly in and strike the coast,
put consciousness into a state of the highest concentration.

I hear the sea, I hear the waves,
each single one counts, and there is never
either one too many or one too few.

Like an almost imperceptible ripple on the water
the desired and the given seem
to change poles, galaxies of hovering thoughts to find rest.

Innocence Italicised

I edge my way into the crannies of your mind,
into narrow rocky clefts where birds
hurl themselves screaming out from high walls of rock.
Between I and I there is no room for anyone else,
you say, but what is between us glows
as a century rises, as waves
when two seas meet, as Skagerrak and Kattegat
move in across each other, as the summer breeze
sweeps through the trees of a long avenue,
so that a trembling propagates itself down among their crowns,
as my yearning and yours, which wants to tear itself away
from a black, screwing depth, but can't.
I press myself to you, in against your heart,
press my lips against your throat, kiss your soul.
That same day you walk through an open gate, irrevocably.

The Sea, I

...I rise up again, I hurl myself forwards,
I stretch myself between continents,
I am without beginning, without end,
and it is not restlessness, when I rend your sleep.
I am in constant motion,
regardless of the changing light, regardless of the air.
I bear my icebergs, I form my coral reefs,
I conceal amphora and floating forests of seaweed,
seethe like boiling tar or lie rockingly quiet,
snake shiny as obsidian in the evening sun,
softly whispering like the smallest children,
who at a distance from the older ones
have come together to play.
Sound my depths and listen to me,
my knowledge stems from the time when
the water under the sky was gathered into one place,
so that the dry land came into view.
I exist from first light until the day darkens,
I brood black at night, lie outstretched
from one end of the world to another.
Above me and all the wellsprings of the earth,
its rivers and streams, its smallest rivulets,
watches the moon, I rise and fall.
Come to me, or I will come to you,
you will not escape me,
just as you cannot be free of the air you breathe,
or hide from the shadow
that follows you as the writing obeys the pen.
If you seek my shores in the surf
I lay bare a ship's hull now and then,
I give what I have gathered,
a scrap of fishing net, a plastic container, a bit of rope,
I come stumbling or dancing in to you
with remains of wreckage or algae-covered timbers
my white wave-crests abruptly raise and hurl away.
I confiscate most of the plunder,
some parts I throw back on the coast again.
Seaweed, mother-of-pearl gleaming shells, jellyfish and starfish
I vomit up in return,

clusters of amber or fossilised creatures
for you, who find instead of seeking.
I turn myself inside out after storms,
roll to and fro with my stones and corpses,
whose names are still being called on land,
but I do not count the graves.
No, there are no survivors on my bed,
I am raw reality, not fiction.
Cutters that spring a leak, and ships that begin to list in storms,
I take with instinctive cascades,
capsized ferries greet my meter-high waves
until I let the victims sleep in my primordial depths.
Light candles for the dead, light candles in the darkness
until all you can see are empty life jackets
and fleets of corpses.
My loud sighs resonate along the shores, I change
from smouldering grey to azure or rustling turquoise,
while my waves beat in against the coast,
rhythmic as a branch against the pane
break into the child's sleep, pounding heavily
like a goods train rolling over the tracks or uncontrollably
as when one who is locked in breaks out of his cell.
I am studied by satellites with magnetic measuring equipment,
I am watched over by patrolling helicopters,
sensitive microphones are lowered into me
to detect microscopic changes,
but I cannot be verified.
I stretch from millions of years
to yet more millions and even further,
lie dazzling as a welding flame,
further than any telescope can see.
Just keep a certainty of mountains over the horizon,
it will be days before you see antipodean land,
you may be blinded by sudden phantom images
or die of thirst on my expanses.
Even where the dry land thinks itself safe, I creep in,
there are places I consume almost imperceptibly
or greedily, when I swallow a cliff,
pull earth and stone and toppling trees with me,
form a gauze-like bandage of foam over the wound.
I can gape further into a coast than you think possible,
I invade bays, find my way into houses,

rinse whitewash from walls, empty cellars
and take with me everything from there, clear storey by storey,
at last making sheer lines totter and buildings collapse,
churches, castles and town halls I take with me in their fall,
I grind rocky coasts to wild sculpture.
Birds that die in mid-song I seize
like burning cosmic detritus, meteors and lost comets,
I glimpse dimly some other falling star
on a spherical path through space.
The wind engraves signs and patterns on my skin,
stamps it like coins of constantly changing value.
Rain and snow and melt water accrue to me,
rivers and water-courses drain themselves into me,
I give off vapour in return.
I am without interruption and without thoughts of flight,
I treasure sandbanks of oysters and conch shells,
a multitude of shellfish open and close in me,
with ornate characters sandworms put down
their daily trails in my interior.
I am filled with tumultuous life
from myriads of microscopically small organisms,
algae and plankton to creatures
the size of the longest ships that cross me.
I rock my fish, I am heavy with
food for animals and people and can fill your nets,
while you stand dreaming on the deck.
I inspect my underground, my hidden pockets
of gas, oil and minerals, my wealth has no boundaries.
I lead ships out of harbours,
send them off in all directions
and usually let them safely back to port again,
fishing boats, cargo ships, battleships,
even colossi of submerged U-boats
spurt in my darkness, from which they soundlessly surface
in order to quickly vanish again, sought by enemy sonar.
Smaller boats with the wind smacking against the sail
and the biggest ships cut through me
as I sparkle under them,
wood, glass fibre and metal carve their way,
but my deep lesions close at once,
the wake subsides, and I am left with no scars.
Ships' prows with figureheads,

dragons, mermaids or spying beauties
cut out like faithful copies of a beloved on land
have ploughed their way through me
and in longing sailed behind others,
but with each ship a trace is wiped out.
Even the smallest dinghy I raised as high
as a father gives his child a ride on his shoulders
across a field or through a wood,
when it no longer has the strength to walk.
Many have gone to sea in order to traverse
my longest and stormiest regions,
where I strike hard and cleave like an axe.
So that their gaze would not get lost on the horizon
they stood on the deck with compass, sextant and map
and charted their position from their course,
at night they followed the stars above me,
inhaling my massive odour of salt.
I wash between Europe and America,
between America, Africa, Australia and Asia,
between North Pole and South Pole.
I am swayingly deep as the cleft
between the amorphous and the animate,
I am without beginning, without end,
I connect continents, or I separate,
depending on whether you master me.
Those who are driven into exile cross me sometimes,
those who travel abroad for pleasure go the same way.
The distance is identical,
the same stars light the way.
I pull myself together and spread myself out,
my voice is mine and no one else's,
by it you know my face.
I rush in towards land and draw myself back again,
listen to my dark vowels and to my light ones,
but my base note is A.
I am the beginning of every language,
I am the essence of them all,
I remember the future and am the key
to secret repositories of meaning.
I call and push away,
from my bosom the sun rises
and dazzlingly refracts the light.

In me the sun sets again
and lets me capture its last darting light,
my murmurings are the particles in the language
that ceaselessly confirms that we are here,
that we talk together, that I listen to you:
'Of course', 'precisely' and 'as you like'.
I struggle obstinately with the gale,
I amuse myself with the sun and the clouds,
conduct nocturnal conversations with the moon and the stars,
a prolonged dialogue, when the ships have lit their lanterns.
I raise no obstacles, I can be travelled over,
the road to the end of the world end passes over me.
That is known by the drunkards who seek their way to the sea
led by sweetly-smelling flowers along the paths
or lured by birdsong from the shrubs.
I can howl like a chained animal,
can drown other voices with my roaring,
bones and skulls of unfortunates who threw themselves out
rattle hidden among sharp-ground stones and rocky reefs.
Small fish swim gaping in and out of the eye-sockets of crania,
first smaller fish, crabs and other small creatures nipped
off the softest and most delicate parts,
eyelids, lips and ears,
then eyes, nose and mouth,
shrimps found their way to all the openings
and found sustenance there,
then the bigger fish arrived and ate,
fish that eat are pernickety.
Crusaders, shipments of slaves,
massacres and robbers' assaults
I have followed at close quarters,
many historic battles have been fought over my fairways,
mired cannons and chains,
mussel-besieged armour and weapons bear witness to them.
Those who fell I have taken to myself,
the killed, the wounded and those who went into shock and collapsed,
those whom with a single wave I hurled overboard,
without names they have acquired the same grave.
I am the waves that chase and disappear,
the waves that say 'and' and 'and' and 'and'.
I carried Noah's Ark, when the source of the world's deeps burst,
and the heavens' sluice-gates opened,

deftly carried the Ark for 150 days and nights,
until the water subsided, and the keel sat on Mount Ararat,
male and female creatures of every species I led securely forth,
while the world's mountains stood under water.
I let Noah and his family go dry-shod to land,
his wife, his sons and son's wives
and then all the animals, two by two.
I am the waves that ceaselessly plane forwards,
I give you the seasons,
the waves that arrive alike, but are different
as people you have met.
I am the waves that roll like a woe, the waves
that rush low like the game chased by dogs,
the waves that make you dizzy or bring forgetfulness.
Nothing can pacify my blood.
I am a holy creature, an infra-wild animal,
on my coasts, close up to the piers
I whisper among the stones, lick them with my long tongue,
greenly they shine when the foam sparkles.
Desire runs darkly in my veins,
I am divinely intoxicated by the light and the air,
and the curse is eternal as the deathly cold in my depths.
I am without beginning, without end,
yesterday is now, now is tomorrow, I am filled
with the holy adrenaline of the adrenal cortex, never find rest.
For every wave I raise I am crowned with the purest white foam
under an unceasing wish to rest
my cheek against another cheek,
feel its warmth and slowly absorb it.
Each wave is a dream, each night a volcanic longing
for someone to throw my arms around, someone to draw to me,
I am for you, what you yourself bring,
I am the sea, I, but my fire cannot be quenched.
As in pain-gleaming fever I lurch
from the grey-white morning light in the horizon
to the strongest sun in the middle of the day,
to muted light, twilight and night.
Above me birds hang screaming,
I am joined to the air forever.
I am the sea, I give you hope for a time,
I rise up again, I hurl myself forwards,
I lie outstretched from one end of the world to another,

I gather the powers of the universe, while you
stand erect between earth and heaven.
I am a mirror for your dreams,
and it is already too late to look away.
I teach you to pray, if you can listen,
my liturgy is understood in every language,
and everyone is chosen –
I show you love, touch you cautiously,
I show you death,
for you will return to the earth or to me,
with me you will find
a dark and mausoleum-quiet depth.
What answer are you looking for?
– There are no questions.
I am without beginning, without end,
glide in between my ice-green walls,
my bosom rises high for you,
sink down into the sucking eddies of my waves,
a tongue of fire will meet you.
I am the mother, the daughter and the worshipped,
the queen who does not abdicate.
Beloved, come to me,
hold me tight, but do not stop me,
the beating of my waves will sound like echoes in your sleep,
but I myself am doomed to never sleep.
I have roots in nothingness,
in me you can be caught and hover like a bird,
I am Heaven and Hell.
With me you are born or die,
indefatigably I give and take.
I am a cavern, I clasp, I hug.

Embraces, eternity...

VI

Vital Liquids

Lacrima

You cannot emigrate
into weeping,
and you cannot remain
camouflaged for long
behind a colourless veil.

I put my arms round you,
I give you my warmth,
listen to the rain
in your eye, it falls
quite by itself.

That is what the tears were like
that watered the earth,
but they are salt,
and after them
nothing grows.

Blood Seconds

Drops of blood burn their way through the snow
with their salt crystal, an opening, a depth of light,
a space that expands without resistance.
Close to is what seems near,
far away: A shot, fleeting fiery colours,
stripes of blood that steaming lead into the forest
where the hunter cannot find the wounded animal,
before the darkness falls, but returns
and is stopped on the path, spitefully stared at by a blind cat.

Blood warms the winter, melts blocks of ice,
the blood in the animal, the blood in the person,
the circling blood of family and friendships.
The heart's prism, the veins' tracery and branchings
in a constant murmur: Why are we here?
What do we want? Where are we going?
Drop-fall. Blood seconds counted by a star,
the body's water is the blood that smells red,
waves that rise in a regulated chaos.

Blood is the present, the time of desire,
the warm touch and the time of blessing.
A horizon of roses planted for the night,
an odour of iron sticks to the sex,
the woman's blood, pure as an unwritten sheet.
There are two kinds of women: Those who swallow
the semen, and those who spit it out –
And there are two kinds of men: Those who lick
a bleeding woman, and those who don't –

The time of fire, the time of earth, the time of air,
the time of blood and water, the time of lovers,
a purling spring, a ceaseless motion.
Taught by an older sister the young girl washes her clothes
in cold water, and it is not a fairytale.
The pulse is counted, world seconds are counted:
The time of fire, the time of earth, the time of air,
the time of blood and persecutions, names
hurled out into frost-cold air are enumerated, one by one.

Countries' borders are not moved with rivers of blood,
just as cities are not built from spilt blood,
blood merely opens the earth's crust to seep down
and only enemies are consoled by blood.
The time of hatred or judgement,
the blood that flows to the final sleep.
An unexpected plummeting of birds, a celestial cobweb
of threads that break, the time of death –
or the light's pale membranes penetrated?

Sweat Hour

The cheeks grow warm, the shoulders, arms and breast grow warm,
and gradually the stomach, legs and feet,
while the barometer visibly rises.

The first drops gather in the face and under the arms,
the dry air stings the nose slightly, there is a prickling in the skin,
pearls drip down the back, the sex grows warm.

The toes move, a restlessness subsides,
and after a while the head
can turn from side to side again without creaking.

The warmth reaches in under the skin,
into the muscles that loosen and grow heavy;
a repose appears, a drowsiness, a sense of well-being.

There is a crackling from the stove, the stones glow, drops move
like the resin that tenaciously flows from the pinewood walls,
all the wrinkles, all the cavities and clefts are wetted.

Drop after drop trickles from the armpits,
the stomach gleams, the jaws relax, parts of the brain switch off,
the nipples stand like faded roses.

It rains from chin and neck, the lips taste of salt,
the back is a rock-face that the water pours down over,
the navel a lake that is filled by warm springs.

The skin sticks, its waste matter is excreted, and the smell
mingles with the fragrances of thirsting pine forests, the sex
opens in the heat, and every leap of thought dwindles in the heights.

Ever further into tissues and bones the heat penetrates,
the throat dries out, the breathing becomes shallow,
the heart beats so alone in the body, that gradually has altered shape.

The sky is low, the eyes and nose burn, there is a twitching in the
          bronchi,
discomfort grows to nausea, until the body sails loose, and the thoughts
have gathered to a sea that can be dried up with a cloth from the floor.

The body, almost immovable as the mountain outside, leaves the sauna,
its fire-red skin is thrown a glance in the mirror, before ready to drop
it staggers by itself through the bathroom like an alphabet drained of
          letters.

The Orchard

*And the earth brought forth grass
and herb yielding seed after his kind, and the tree
yielding fruit, whose seed was in itself, after his kind*
GENESIS 1.12

Bite into an apple whose skin
is covered with moisture and cold.
It hung like a pendulum in the morning breeze,
a growth stopped in the midst of its counting.
I swung in through a hole in the hedge,
under the tree's crown, turned
the fruit round on its stem,
before it fell into others' hands
or ended as drops
in the beaks of passing birds.

The odour is slightly sour under the nose,
I bite hard on the apple, so the saliva leaps
from the glands under my tongue, from jaws and cheeks.
The dew celebrates my thirst,
and the day that ripens,
while the tongue strays soundlessly
in its wet darkness, as fire consumes straw,
climbs over the white flesh
with quick smacks between teeth and palate.

Bit into the apple so the juice spurted,
and the orchard's owner saw that it was good.
I ran after the light, which like the water
gushed from the earth, up
through the tree and out into its fruit.
I seized an apple from the most beautiful tree,
where the worms were also taking theirs.
I plucked freely, banished to myself,
left the orchard clear-sighted
and hungry as never before.

Inscription

Between night and morning on the way home across the shore
you step out on large, algae-covered stones at the edge of the water.
And bathed in the moon's radiance, with your back
to me, you piss in the sea
with a sound so tinklingly pure and with resonance,
from the time the boys wrote their names
with steaming yellow in the snow, and we,
from a swing in motion, replied
with an even longer sparkling stream,
with flying, hot drops, later
in turns to conquer by being submissive:
With a flicker in our eyes of lunatic delight
sluice one another in tickling torrential rain of mighty lakes
and then see the weeds grow strangely liberated, dead-nettle
and ground elder grown gigantic in size, where we,
swathed in a light metaphysically wet,
had in secret left our sweet, stinking animal tracks.

June Dream

The morning you are to arrive, I rise from sleep,
it is June, and I go naked,
heavily swaying over the floor, no different
from those cows that waddle to meet me
when on mild evenings I appear at the fence on the meadow;
I am awake and ready,
the first rays of light flood in
across my belly's pointed cupola, the throne
from which you long have reigned wildly and autocratically.

The water seeps warmly down along thigh and knee,
down to my calves, over my feet, out on to the floor,
I hear the sound of a brook far away, a clear
and silent whispering between moss-grown stones;
am thrown deep into myself when the pains roll in:
Three suns of snow and a star of fear,
dive under the sea and am carried back
in an arc across a golden bridge:
You are born only once –

Marvel from a distant planet at the howl
you extend the walls with as a greeting
to the world that waits in white morning mist,
I lift you up, look into your eyes, which I know,
but have never met,
try to understand what they ask about,
lose blood, but let your first morning
be filled with light, with caresses and prophetic dreams,
talk to you and say:

One day you will walk yourself, and life is yours, my son,
the earth that turns is for you, gardens of flowers
with thousands of colours and only one serpent you must watch out for,
jungles, deserts and endless plains of motley animals,
fields with sprouting seeds in spring, in autumn you may hunt game,
forests of labyrinthine adventures and tall trees to climb,
mountain ranges with ravines and sparkling minerals,
a burning sky with clouds and swarms of birds,
oceans of fish and treasure chests from lost ships.

Snow, rain and other stainless mirrors
in which year by year you can see yourself grow,
cities that will lure and light your way, and when you grow older:
Concert halls that keep the fear away,
a princess who will let her tongue play in your mouth,
long before you manage to say something stupid
– and to the great, empty space
that has overwhelmed others before you,
you can then direct your questions.

Antidote

Through the night the milk runs
in subterranean sparkling gland-passages.
White swans on their way
across the water
in outstretched peace.

Children drink under restless clouds
only interrupted by the stillness,
as though they were draining the tree of its sap.
And in dreams
the grown men also steal
from my breasts.
Not to still their hunger,
but to be able
to die better.

A wave of light sways
and washes over them,
a scent of wild growing apples,
an antidote to the poison,
while they listen to the heartbeat's
millennial change.
They drink, they get up,
continue their struggle
against a tireless enemy,
ravage and wrench apart
what was born close-seamed...

VII

The Bath

The Angel Is Having Its Feet Washed

The angel is having its feet washed,
it has gone around barefoot
and has entered the house by accident, like an insect.

Everyone else fled in all directions
when it stepped inside,
as if the fire had got too close to them.

For a long time I had heard someone calling,
but of fear
the one who feels fear cannot speak.

This world is also a planet
for angels,
now one is sitting exalted and upright before me.

I have let my hair down,
brought in a tub of water
and brushed the heavenly dust from its feet.

If love can be considered from a bird's perspective
it is not love
but something else.

The sun falls in a moment of grace in through the window,
I notice the ripped soles of the angel's feet,
as long as I'm washing, I won't scream.

The Child Learns to Love Water

The child is unwrapped from his robes and lowered
slowly, to gentle humming,
softer than the cat carries her kitten by the scruff of its neck,
down into his first bath, tepid
as in caves and lagoons, as inside the dome of the womb.

A lake is given, a river, a sea –

A gaze hunts around, finds its mooring-place in mine,
the peace of wonder spreads,
something that could be mistaken for reflectiveness
– this is also an element:
Kick and start, water splashes up over the edge of the tub.

A world before language is given, a universe to frolic in –

A kiss on the child's forehead, warm rain through the hair
from a hollowed hand, and over the body water is poured quietly,
the cloth slides over breast and neck and further round,
a clenched hand is straightened out, fingers are rinsed,
while the child floats, hovers lightly.

Stems, sepals, petals of newly fallen snow –

The child up again,
the child through the cold air,
the child packed in terry cloth & dabbed dry,
the child made a fuss of, looked at & admired,
the child kissed on the stomach, the child caressed & in his clothes.

Some shall conquer, others bleed; it is all against all, war without
    mercy –

Out of My Sleeping Form

Turn the tap on, still walled round by sleep,
with an instinctive twist.
Find my way under the shower as turtles find the sea,
streams of warmth creep around me,
as I am covered by a floating sea of drops.
Jerk all at once from before to now, from yesterday to today,
to the milestone of this moment.

An encroachment on space is a gate, a tempting weight,
an exhortation to leave, an exhortation to go in,
as the morning is a sloping road, I must pass
alone,
a hesitation, a decision, a gorge of light
and on the other side of the gate:
– The not-known, which with a peculiar lightness welcomes me.

Down over me the water spreads in a radiating spin,
of finely branching tentacles.
I wash the night away, wash human skin
to the clearest sky, from tiredness to suppleness
the distance is only a few minutes.
I turn under a vertical flood, hold my breath
and lift my face toward the softly rustling jets.

As the drops fall, and the room is filled with hot steam,
as the water streams through my hair and down over my body,
does it cure all the wounds of reality,
as if it possibly were the origin of every living thing?
I wash myself and wake up slowly,
for a brief moment to draw myself into further silence,
a bride in a veil of foam.

The fever breath of the walls, drops thick and fast against the scalp,
my brain surpassed by ever more flights of birds,
for each inner pinprick
a thought grows prismatically,
reaches obelisk height.
Observe which way the water screws down,
the same way the planet turns.

My eyes seek upwards, the sky is dark
behind the dewed panes.
I step out of the morning's primordial mists, out
of my sleeping form, naked
and fragrantly warm, clad only in a net of shiny drops.
Drip through the room
a glowing stripe of stars across the floor.

I must be clean,
as I stamp snow and gravel from my boots
before I enter a house.
Flying clean, as I step into a new day,
perhaps to the square root of a rose,
where someone plunges
to caress its wealth of folds, drink its sun.

Flaming Water

...and he looked like a god as he came from the bath
HOMER

A bath I will give you, as Circe's maids bathe Odysseus,
like those daughters of the groves and the fountains
and of the holy rivers that run down to the sea,
I fill the bath with water and pour you wine.

I mix in a jet hot water with some that is cooling,
while the mirrors mist over, and silence comes creeping;
a long bath you shall have, the wine will illumine your blood
and loosen those muscles I rinse with water from a jug.

As the fourth maid drove the weariness out of Odysseus's limbs,
I shall bathe you, so that the world for a time narrows down to this room,
where mild vapours are yielded ever more densely, and your skin's
          fragrances
expand in the room as warmth fills you, both from outside and in.

I move closer, wash your neck and your chest,
caress your face, your nape and your shoulders,
notice delight trickle forth as I see you forget your weapons,
see you let all your limbs relax and sink further down in the bath.

There must be water so that there is life,
and men need long baths...
I soap you and rinse you again, your body grows heavy,
you are not just one man, but many men.

And when you stand up in the bath to emerge,
you are no less charming than Telemachus,
who was bathed by the lovely maiden Polycaste,
before he was anointed with glistening oil and covered with shirt and
          mantle.

Whose is the love that shines through the world like a running river,
and why does it flow pure as a soul
that comes towards me, so different from anything I have met
in the maze of the palace where I wandered so long alone.

The Merciless

Verily I have cleansed my heart in vain,
and washed my hands in innocency.
For all the day long have I been plagued,
and chastened every morning!

PSALMS, 73. 13

Under a gushing tap I scrub earth from my hands,
clayey lumps are softly loosened in the warm jet.
Soap my hands and remember in the whirls of foam a woman
standing in front of a hand basin, rubbing her face with soap,
her cheeks, the wings of her nose, and chin; she rinses her mouth,
       spits out,
soaps her hands and lower arms carefully, she sluices the foam away,
pays attention neither to herself nor others in the mirror.

Like waking sleep are her movements, as feathers flicker
on their way down through the air, without birds being seen in the sky.
The foam grows tall, it gleams and is dissolved by the water,
but the merciless sticks and cannot be rinsed away
like the earth I long ago got off my hands.

A sorrow between the tiles, a cold like the shiny metal of the taps,
a point of gravity moved, a fear that has possessed a soul.
I spray water on the tub, watch the last remains of mud float away,
turn the water off and dry my hands,
while the woman mechanically tries to free herself from an unknown act,
sinking further into her own silent darkness, her heart
will never become white, and no bird will alight on her shoulder.

Grey

A wind like shattered glass from mountains with ice and snow,
an Icelandic day as naked as a bone
gnawed free of flesh, so creakingly cold
that the key breaks in its lock,
at the far end of the rock in long wooden stands
the sound of fine blows on thin porcelain,
a quiet, hollowly rolling tinkling
from long rows of dried fish, the winter is flowering.

Rather than being wrapped in a fur-lined coat
I will let myself glide down into the water from the warm springs
to morning-bathe under a Nordic sky,
keep my head cold, but be swathed in the warmth
and float in emptiness under clouds that part;
it is best to wake up in water,
when the dreams' seven-league boots
have been kicked far under the bed.

Get up in the wind that has stroked
across the frost-hardened earth, move
to warmer tubs and let myself sink deeper,
when the body has grown used to the temperature,
lean my neck back and stare down into a cloud crater,
exchange one thought with another,
replace the circle with its square
like changing children grown in me.

Inhale the pale blue, greyish sky, a daily dose
radiates out to the slightest cavities in the lungs,
in one suck dispelling pain and its echo,
I open myself to the chains of mountains,
to the valleys and the plains, I listen
to the birds' first notes:
The beak that one moment opens to sing,
pecks the next in warm manure.

Ice Age

You shall be clean in death,
like sweeping winter wind
amidst naked December branches,
when your body is robbed of its soul,
you shall be washed again, as if you were a little child.

You shall be washed without knowing by whom,
probably by strangers,
the sweat of fear shall be rubbed away, the skin transformed
to a sky of glass over the heart, the black bird
that stopped in mid flight.

They will bring a washtub and wet cloths,
they will stroke your powerless limbs, touch you
as only close kinsmen in a distant past dared,
smothered in your sleep you will meet the water
without noticing if it is cold or scalding hot.

They won't need to dip their elbows in the tub,
as they did when you were an infant,
to make sure the temperature was right,
before the cloth slid intimately over your body
into all its folds and fissures.

You shall have your fingers straightened,
your nails cleaned and clipped,
both those on toes and on fingers,
you will have your hair combed
and your eyebrows plucked.

Regardless of whether your mind was blamelessly pure,
they will wash you and dress you in white,
so that you will be clean in death,
white as you perhaps from dizziness never wore,
you will be dressed by unknown hands.

Long shall your tracks smell of wild animal,
after the sound of your steps has vanished,
but you will look like a bride
when you leave this world again,
a born bride with frozen veins.

You will not hear the fire from the other side,
your flood of images stopped long ago,
and the language you have won
lies like a kingdom
you have left behind you.

A light as from the winter sun will radiate from you,
when they have got you ready,
you will perhaps cast a blue, almost invisible shadow;
in your coffin, lined with snow and cold as a church,
you can travel in peace, their age remains your ice age.

VIII

The Rain

Rain Sum

Even before it flows, the rain can be heard
like the distant echo of a waterfall,
the animals in the fields become restless,
then the drops come.

Thick as a horse's mane they fall,
irradiate the greenness,
thin-skinned leaves quiver under hard blows,
young birds press together, tufted with down.

From the whole rainy sky I catch single drops,
then multiply them into the rest,
the way the word 'casualty-figures' only gains meaning
when a friend is lost or a beloved.

Fear that a flickering second
keels over into a life-long shadow;
may his light shine like the words
in a sentence before it runs out.

In order to be completed
in its own disappearance,
become one with the soil
that gives language its food.

Whistling

The greenness, the drops on the forest floor
after the rain, the drops in moss and maidenhair,
the tall grass, the wet summer,
where the bird has a nest and the fox a lair.
It whistles in the trees, whistles in my head,
it sparkles, rushes, cold, hot, cold,
the drops tight in the leaf, it gleams, flashes,
when I touch the wetness, shake the branches,
spread the shine, the wild glitter
that pours out of me too, heavy with light.
I open my mouth, stick out my tongue,
feel the wet, the star-coloured,
it whistles in the trees, whistles in my head,
the high summer, the wild grass,
your rain-wet taste, your raw fragrant rain,
I sink to the ground in the dark blazing greenness,
in a wedge birds rise high above the trees.

Lesson Behind the Leaves

Closed is the school where nightingales daily
rehearse songs that only a wakening love
later makes them masters in.
The birds sit caught behind a skewed trellis of needles,
wings folded together for the rain.

The drops shine, meet the leaves and the earth in cold stabs
or roll down across the pane, hour after hour.
The drops strike the roof, colour the notes
that sing behind one's temple,
all the hours wound; the last kills.

Summer in Denmark. On Location

Sudden darkness
and wind
taking hold through the open window.

With a flash of lightning the sky
is emptied of birds, in a gust of wind
they are all sent away.

A roll of thunder cleaves the sky,
low-hovering clouds
swell and gape black.

Lightning again
splitting the clouds,
rain falls, hard and vertical.

Lightning –
under steady torrential rain,
branches bow deep towards the earth.

Lightning –
birdsong ceases from bushes and trees,
rain, drizzling rain, driving rain.

Lightning –
rain like a humming from thousands of boisterous brains,
the thunder crashes, moves on.

Lightning –
the rain sluices dust from the leaves, scrubs
like dancing brooms the hot roofs of the city.

Lightning –
the sky grey, grey, almost blind,
the street emptied of people for a while.

Lightning –
even in here a deep sea darkness,
so that the book cannot be read.

Lightning –
and gradually the sound of raincoats,
hymns against unfurled umbrellas.

Lightning –
the rain fills forgotten bottomless jars,
wipes out gothic castles in kindergarten sandpits.

Lightning –
thunder and cars ploughing through lakes in the streets,
a roar of rain, the air an impenetrable mist.

Lightning –
a boy strokes a finger through the drops
on a parked BMW, caresses the shine.

Lightning –
a girl sticks her hand in where a drain pipe
has broken, plays with the foaming water.

A rumbling further away, lightning flashes illumine the sky,
then peal follows peal, keeping the dying
awake for some time yet.

And measured by these elementary forces
the city's anger is just a spark that is quenched,
an ignited madness effaced with a forgiving reply.

Ever more arrows, lightning –
hurrying across the sky
and making the bones glitter.

Another detonation
at which the panes rattle, another flash –
that could split a tree from crown to foot.

More torrential rain, more lightning –
tearing down the sky, cascade of cataracts,
every sluice is opened, crevices, holes and cracks are filled.

The rain stops,
lightning follows lightning –
smaller reports like the voices of pistols.

Another boom, more lightning –
misty drizzle, the rain breaks loose again,
turns into ropes to climb to the sky on.

The thunder moves away,
rolls onward, but new claps
sound shortly after right over this house, lightning –

It is summer, lightning –
and wild-growing darkness, sudden night in the midst of day,
a moment's stillness, lightning –

The pealing comes again, the rain starts again,
flashes in quick succession –
in the rain all men look like my old lovers.

Heavy rumbling and more blaring,
pouring rain, living time,
on the balcony further away, washing forgotten on a line,

A ceaseless drumming on the roofs,
a gurgling from the depths,
water-rats gnaw their way from below.

Blinking lightning, smaller claps,
the rain is growing, again a gigantic peal,
persistent gleaming.

The rain goes on for a long time,
falls still and stops, the air cleansed
the confused thoughts of recent days brought to a cease.

Dripping from the roofs, dripping from the trees in the street,
rainy mist and wet, muddy animals,
paddling sounds, saturated smells.

The thunder rolls away, out across the sea,
many-coloured clearing
– a portal of birds' warbling.

Only a Knife

We have drunk of the poisoned water
and are visited by the contagion:
You walk in like a stranger,
talk to me like someone I don't know,
the windows are wide open to winter.
Like a long night's sleep
a wing will brush through the opening,
streak from the sky into the innermost,
nearly invisible corners.
It will get inexorably cold,
but my pulse beats, I survive
like a frost-rose embedded in snow.
No one has wounded me as ruthlessly as you,
yet only a freshly sharpened knife
can cut us free of each other.
It will rain again, fever-deep
I will ignite your body, which I know
down to the most finely drawn veins,
your face will turn towards me,
as the earth sails with us.
It will rain, and the sand
be rinsed from your eyes.
I curse not old age,
but the blindness
with which even those who can see
move about.
It will rain, and my caresses
will make you draw your breath, as you do
when with tenderness you annul my weight,
there where we shall never meet
and therefore never part either.

The Heavenly Spire

The spire in the middle of town pricks holes in the cloud,
a sleeping colossus hung up on its own weight,
lead-dark and suddenly close, a mountain overturned at the root.

It rains life-givingly: First hesitating in gleams and splashes of light,
then the sky gathers into a convulsive grey light,
and the water strikes like a haemorrhage, steam rises.

The trees in the parks drink, the lakes drink, the grass
and the trampled paths drink, roof gutters and drain pipes
drink, basins, bowls, an abandoned cup.

A thousand voices stretch the city out in a murmur
of condensed time, sounds slash between the houses
as if from sharp weapons, the flood of traffic is halted.

The sky in a steep jump towards the depths
that sucks the last light of space
like eyes sunk into their sockets.

From where a gaze is sensed dully, like the reflex death
from its shelter now and then can send up
from the earth's interior in remembered shocks of cold.

In a few minutes the water rises above gutters and flagstones
further up between the houses, until the noise drowns,
and the city lies like an open watery grave.

A boat tears itself free of its moorings,
glides out in light and carries you slowly away,
while you hear birds sing in your sleep.

Sail on, sentenced to stillness your pulse beats loudly,
and the newborn girl you in dreams first suckle
and then lay in the wet earth, you call Mole.

The Soul's Lake

A wave of cold washes through my brain,
shivering I watch the sun disappear.
The loss is so heavy I can't weep.
My eyes are dry with mourning, smarting and sore,
my tears are not tears, just something
that cuts, something that burns instead.
But you have not wanted
the world to dry out like an insect,
because you have left it.
The air curls, I drive alone, when the weather changes,
I kill the engine, listen to the rain's prelude:
Drops fall like pearls across a floor
from a necklace, when the thread breaks; pearls
that are scattered cannot be gathered again,
but plunge finally into the roar of cataracts.
The drops strike ever thicker,
whirling rivers behind time.
Keep in to the side in order to hear the rain
drum on the roof of the car,
flash after flash dazzles and illuminates the forest.
Sit quite still at the wheel
in the growing darkness...
I willingly go to meet the rain
as it cleaves the air, and the night stands open,
as I went to meet you
or was it you who came to me,
your words that transfixed me
like the showers of rain that are coming just now
– the men who bat themselves to stay warm in the cold,
why were they hugging themselves,
I had the warmth, wanted to go in
between their strong arms –
The sky full of drops, a swarming nothing
like the unwritten sheet of paper once between us.
The rain knows no walls, it's raining here,
and it may rain in other places at the same time,
or the rain may move
like a wave across the planet,

make plants drill their way up, twist their way out
of the smallest cracks in the rock,
make dry brushwood break out into thorny green
in the sun-hot sand of the most desolate desert,
make the most inhabitable regions habitable.
The rain does not lie, the rain transforms,
as those plunging torrents now build
a house of silence around me,
so that I shall not drown in emptiness.
I have drunk and drunk of the rain
until my eyes shine, I have bathed in it,
have let it caress me, press
its burning cold kisses to my forehead...
The lightning stops, the rain floats away,
is absorbed into the realm of plants, the realm of beasts.
The sky plays with the earth, I listen
to the water and think differently about you now,
listen to the pulse of the deepest springs:
The water shall flow through the poems of the world.

IX

The Rainbow

Marriage

The drop marries the lake,
that marries the river,
where we bathe or strew ashes
of our dead.
Each word is a farewell,
and the words spawn, as the tree
unfolds its leaves.
Each day a loss, a farewell
to a country, a farewell
to a voice's whirlpool.
My centre is no different
from the rain's, it is
where you place your kisses,
all over my body.
The river marries the sea,
that marries the rain,
that marries infinity,
a shining thread, an umbilical cord
through which the blood courses, red
as pomegranate seeds
spun from the body, from us
who must constantly consider:
Why?
From us where questions
in all the colours of the rainbow live.

Disarmed

Unless I am mistaken at a distance here by the tall gravestones,
in snow that falls stilly, burying the graves,
those are grown men playing by the spruce trees
in the gateway between earth and heaven.

At the Jewish cemetery in Berlin,
where gardeners are employed to tend the graves, to cheerful cries
they are rolling large balls of snow along the paths:

There must be snowmen
to cheer the dead
– and living.

So we don't need to cautiously sneak about,
we are permitted to carve our laughter, an orange glow,
into this dark darkness, light a lantern
and let it swing in the twilight over Prenzlauer Berg.

Illuminated Night

Naked we are thought in between the stones of the world,
skeletons with about two hundred bones,
bilaterally, symmetrically constructed,
joints, muscles, vessels, nerves,
organs that consume, organs that secrete,
organs that try to separate the true
from its skin, mortal parts attached to an astral brain
that does not forget the oldest rituals.
And water, more water than land are we, seventy percent,
over which a rainbow-like soul
from its shelter illumines us from inside.
Creations whose sleep can be punctuated by fear
that wavers out into each blind corner
in a feverish trembling,
a filtered root network geometrically illegible
to the one who delights in the peaceful tree.
Creatures that can suddenly make a misty sorrow vanish
to drown in one another.
Bodies, that between south pole and north pole
like waves in a millennia-dazed ocean
rise up against one another in cold abysmal nights
to form a gate together,
a secret passage.
Unarticulated is love when without a scenario
or other commands it wells forth
releasing the sounds with which we light the stars,
so rivers of yellow light flow out into the universe.

No Way Back

Already before the words are thought
they come travelling from far away,
lie in the oral cavity shut in by a tongue
that blocks the exit like a stone,
I don't know the words, only notice that they have direction.

With the strength of a glacier they press their way forward,
but don't get past the barrier of the lips,
they are so big that in front of a mirror
– while the light stands still –
I clip the corner of my mouth with a long paper-scissors.

From the moment I make the incision with exactitude
and feel the metal passing through my skin,
my mouth opens as on fish
that look like old, tired men, greybeards
moving agape in an oceanic darkness.

What is born comes out of a mouth,
and there is no way back, there are only
mind-steps to climb, and there are gateways for everything;
I force my jaws open,
my lips are numb with pain.

Dry stones lose smell and fire,
don't have the same essence as when water sluices over them
making the colours sprout in their fulsome brilliance,
no different from the tongue
when it has roots in its own language.

From bark and leaves the fragrance floats saturated,
if the trees stand wet after a rain shower,
like the words, before they again are subject to their vanishing,
hover most clearly in the room after a glass of water,
when lips, palate and tongue are refreshed.

I take a gulp of the water,
open my mouth so fatally wide
that even the biggest words can pass,
the pain wears off,
the wound slides over into green and yellow.

Now one follows these lips
in order gaping and more visibly to remember
how cries from a subterraneanly sliding depth
are gracefully distilled and suddenly transformed
into a rainfall of living words.

From the Coral Abyss

The newly in love cannot escape each other,
one caress glides imperceptibly
into the next; let go.

I drink of the juice
from the autumn's cryingly
bitter green grapes,
while ebb and flow
measure out the dreams' hidden wishes.

Tears borne by laughter,
Elysian rain
or the rainbow's mating colours
handed down in a straight line, reveal
that not all is determined by reason.

The cat has carefully
split a pile
of fallen birds' feathers
to share out the goods;
now the house looks like a madhouse for angels.

And why it is necessary
to lie awake
in shifting pain positions, quivering
with moonlight in one's heart
to write these wildly flying lines
– strew a path
of shining salt-grains in the dark –
deep down there in my brain's
coral abyss I cannot possibly
find an answer to, but I do,
as with peace of mind I submit myself to other laws of nature.

The Dreams' Watering Place

Those who have ears to hear
will discern an ocean of sounds,
an undersea current of words
gliding up from the darkness and flying away
with a memory of clouds,
of shadows, of rivers' hurtling
and the wind through the grass.
The fish's silk-fine, transparent fins,
a tail-fin, a dorsal and anal fin,
two ventral fins and two gill-fins,
seven wings to travel at the speed of blood
through the seas of the world
from night to night
among dolphin skulls, petrified snails
and fossilised oysters, among green algae
which glow during the day like an eternal spring.
Seven colours in a rainbow
to fly across the sky
like the year's first roe-deer
leaping across the fields.
Seven colours in a rainbow
geometrically pulled
across the soul's firmament,
long before the oldest vertebrates
populated the water, an era
before the first went up on land
and then gave life to amphibians,
to crawling reptiles, birds and finally to the one
who now sits perfectly still, listening.
Those who have eyes to see with
should listen well
when the rain falls, when the drops
sound like the light in music,
pure as the boy's first emission of semen
and not least afterwards
when an acoustic rainbow
among rocky massifs and mountain peaks
delicately burning rises from the dust,

hurtling upwards,
and in a blue pulsing gleam
your head swims with love for your life,
because it is yours
and knows that it closes
as the gate to this poem
slams shut now.

Seal

No, it is not a secret, like the one that is hidden
behind a sleeper's closed eyes, not an ingenious code,
which we long pretend to carry around, handed down
from grandparents or parents on their deathbeds.

It is a vibration in the muscles left by a chronic restlessness
that causes ripples even on this summer day,
where the wind has died, and wild scents from still dripping
bushes and flowers weightlessly strike roots in the warm air.

It is a force and counter-force, it is a pain woken to life,
an inner intifada, a new stone age of the mind, where I am taken
          prisoner
by myself, for I don't think behind bullet-proof glass, when I go that
          way
everyone can only go alone, when I waken a language, a queen's realm.

I find a system of paths, move across bridges or out of gateways,
I travel towards an outermost limit, go through dreamlike passages,
give my voice – the rest I lose like the blood from a violet opened vein;
the earth draws everything to it and drinks, afterwards smells damp
          with rain.

Over the words a rainbow sets its glowing seal.

NOTES

The Queen's Gate: During my second stay in Jerusalem in connec-
tion with the genesis of *Territorial Song*, on the 21st of May 1993
I had the following experience: I was walking through the Arabian
quarter, which is always densely packed with men. The few women
to be seen wear veils, and in recent years many have begun to cover
their faces again. I continued my walk to Mea She'arim, the quarter
of the ultra-orthodox Jews. Here I first succeeded in being seen as
a devil by one man, while another, as he was stepping out of the
synagogue, burst out: 'Oh, no!', whereupon he turned away because
I had evidently been too close to the men's entrance. In the Bukara
Quarter I tried to look into a synagogue that had opened its doors.
Here an old gentleman came towards me and asked: 'Do you seek
troubles?' Once again I had come too close to the men's entrance.
I asked where the women's one was, but it was closed... In a con-
tinuation of the experiences of that day, I reflected that in the wall
around the old part of the city of Jerusalem not one of the eight gates
referred to anything female: Jaffa Gate, New Gate, Damascus Gate,
Herod's Gate, St Stephen's Gate, Golden Gate, Dung Gate and
Zion Gate. St Stephen's Gate is also known as Lion's Gate (in
Hebrew Sha'ar Ha'araiot, and the Arabs call it Bab Sitt Miriam,
the Mary Gate), but the English names I came across did not
denote anything female. My idea then was that there must be a
way into the world for women, too. *Queen's Gate*, I called it.

It also struck me that in ancient theatre the stage consisted of a
palace. The façade was made of marble and had a gate in the middle,
a king's gate. Two smaller gates were sited symmetrically in the
wings. The classical frame could be used as a palace, temple or
market place. The fixed scenery made it possible for any ancient
tragedy to be performed here. A king's gate on its own is not
sufficient for a modern drama, however – here a queen's gate
would also be required. When the work on my previous book
Territorial Song was finished, I wanted to write such an entrance
So this book was called *The Queen's Gate*, a year before it was
begun... 'Queen' in the poetic sense of the word.

Hatshepsut in Memoriam: Hatshepsut was an Egyptian queen
of the 18th dynasty in the 15th century BC. Regent for her stepson
Thotmes III during his minority.

Wansee: A district of Berlin. The conference at which Reinhard Heydrich at Goering's request presented the proposal for a 'solution' of the so-called 'Jewish problem' was held here. 'Die Endlösung' was ready on 20 January 1942. At the villa Am Grossen Wannsee the top brass of the Nazi party and the involved part of the SS leadership met in order to plan and organise a purge of all the Jews in Europe.

The Profile of Memory: The Latin quotation comes from Tycho Brahe, who accompanies two alchemistic vignettes with the following texts: 'suspiciendo despicio' (as I look up, I look down), and 'despiciendo suspicio' (as I look down, I look up).

Flaming Water: Lines from Homer's *Odyssey* are woven into this poem.

Seal: a greeting to Gunnar Ekelöf.